RV LIVING

100+ Amazing Tips, Secrets, Hacks & Resources to Motorhome Living

Kevin Moore (C)2015

Disclaimer:

This book is for informational purposes only and the author, his agents, heirs, and assignees do not accept any responsibilities for any liabilities, actual or alleged, resulting from the use of this information.

This report is not "professional advice." The author encourages the reader to seek advice from a professional where any reasonably prudent person would do so. While every reasonable attempt has been made to verify the information contained in this eBook, the author and his affiliates cannot assume any responsibility for errors, inaccuracies or omissions, including omissions in transmission or reproduction.

Any references to people, events, organizations, or business entities are for educational and illustrative purposes only, and no intent to falsely characterize, recommend, disparage, or injure is intended or should be so construed. Any results stated or implied are consistent with general results, but this means results can and will vary. The author, his agents, and assigns, make no promises or guarantees, stated or implied. Individual results will vary and this work is supplied strictly on an "at your own risk" basis.

Table of Contents

Introduction

The open road. For many of us, a life spent traveling and adventuring into the great unknown feels like a thing possible only in dreams. Well, I'm here to share with you that it's much closer in reach then you'd think. In this book, I'm going to share with you all the tips, tricks and resources I've learned over the past few years. Hopefully, you won't be forced to go through many of the same growing pains I had to experience while pursuing a life of RV living full time.

For some getting a RV means the ability to free themselves from a life chained down to one spot. For others it's the ability to stop paying a mortgage and live a modest life of travel and leisure. Whatever the reason is, RV living offers a little something for everyone.

I want to extend to you my sincerest thanks for purchasing my book. I started my journey three years ago, and it has been nothing short of a life altering experience. I went from working a mind numbing 50+ hours a week and traveling once a year with my family, to seeing every state except Hawaii, as well as making my way across a good part of Canada.

The best part is not only did I see these places but I got to stay there, and experience them. When you're on the road, there is no ticking clock, or plane home you need to catch. If you like a particular place, stay there for an extra few weeks, hell, some people I've met along my journeys hunker down in one spot for months at a time, before moving on to the next. There is no wrong amount of time to spend!

Now, I don't want to sugarcoat the RV lifestyle. While it is amazing, I do want to stress, there's a ton of work and planning that needs to be done before cutting the cord, and hitting the open road. Preparation and research in the initial phases will serve you well for the months and years to come.

I hope you're excited to get started, let the journey begin!

Chapter One: The Initial Phase – Finding a RV That's Right For You

In this section, you will find:

- The Importance of Goal Setting

- Questions You Need to Answer Before Buying

- Where to Rent and Buy a RV

- Some Key Features to Consider

The Importance Of Goal Setting

One of the main issues new RV full timers face is that they didn't take some time to map out what they needed in advance, and are left without it, or left scrambling to try and find it. Goal setting is an important tool you can use in order to achieve the things you want out of life. Remember, goal setting only truly works if you have the desire to create change. If you're setting goals just to set them, you're wasting time.

I suggest you write out of list of your goals before getting started. Once you know what you're trying to get out of the RV lifestyle, you'll be better equipped to find ways to make it happen. Personally, I set new goals for myself each year. These goals are fluid, and they often change or get altered depending on new experiences, needs, or wants.

Questions You Need to Answer Before Buying

In this section I've compiled a few questions every newbie should answer before purchasing a RV and heading out.

Congrats! You've decided to join the growing ranks of individuals leaving their life behind and are determined to hit the open road. Do yourself a favor and answer these questions before making your next move. The more questions you know the answer to in advance, the better decisions you'll be able to make come purchase time.

- Are you going to RV full time or RV part time?

- What is your budget for the RV?

- How will your savings look after purchasing a RV?

- Are you going to work from the road to earn additional cash?

- If so, what kind of job do you plan on working?

- Are you looking for a towable RV, or are you looking for a motorized RV?

- What size and class RV do you need? What are your storage requirements?

- Have you gotten your license upgraded, and attended any courses on RV safety?

- Do you know the legal considerations regarding operating a RV?

- What RV features are a must need, and what RV features are wants?

- Have you figured out a monthly road budget, or estimated monthly expenses?

- What are you going to do with your current residence? If you own, are you going to sell or rent out your property?

- How do you plan to send and receive mail?

- Are you going to place your stuff in long term storage, or sell and give it away?

- Have shopped around for estimated prices on RV insurance plans, or RV roadside assistance plans?

As you can tell there are a lot of important questions that need to be answered before leaving. There will many more questions to ask yourself along the way, but these are a few you'll want to think over before making that initial purchase.

Where to Rent and Buy a RV

Once you finished the first two processes I mentioned above, it's time to start your search in earnest. Take it from me, you want to rent before you buy. I would schedule a few weekend trips with different class RV models, and different feature sets, in order to give you a broad idea of what you want while out on the road. You'll find some of the things you thought are important, really aren't. You'll also find the opposite to hold true.

This is essentially going to be your new home, only on wheels. When you went house or car shopping you didn't buy site unseen, you checked each property, or car out and did your research. With RV's not only is the interior important but you've got to be comfortable driving it all over the country, across every terrain imaginable. If it looks pretty but is a nightmare to drive, you're going to be unhappy, and the whole point of the RV living is to get the most enjoyment out of life.

Here is a list of some the top places you can rent a RV:

Cruise America RV Rentals

Recreation Vehicle Rental Association Rentals By State

Canada RV Rentals

All Motorhome Rental

Blue Travel RV Rentals

Bates International Motorhome Rentals

Oregon RV Rentals

Colorado Camper Rentals

El Monte RV Rentals

Road Bear RV Rentals

Moturis RV & Motorcycle Rentals

RV Rentals Of Orlando

Texas RV Owners' Rentals

Neff Brothers RV Rentals In Ohio

Still looking for more places to rent a RV try these two sites for more options:

RV Net Linx

RV Zone

Once you've had the opportunity to rent a RV, take it out on the road, and actually experience the RV life a little, you'll have a clearer understanding of what you require in a RV. Many of you will want to jump right in and skip renting first, but I hope you reconsider. The last thing you want when making a large purchase is regret.

So you've done all your homework and you're finally ready to buy. The only question left is where to buy from.

Here are a list of some of the top places to buy a RV:

RV Trade Shows – Hands down my favorite way to shop for a RV. First off, you get a ton of RV's in one place, sporting all the latest features. On top of that, you also get representatives of many of the top RV manufacturers, who are willing to answer any questions you may have.

RV Dealerships – Not as much inventory, and you have to deal with sales people trying to pressure you into a sale. Otherwise, if you have a firm idea of what you want this is a good way to pick out your new RV

RV Manufacturers – I've never done this personally, but I've had a few of my friends who are fellow travelers purchase their motorhomes this way. They all seemed quite pleased with the experience.

RV Trader – This is my top pick if you're looking to find a RV online. A lot of options to choose from.

RVT – Another large online site, however not the size of RV Trader.

RV Registry - Has a good amount of online inventory.

Classy RV – Online site with decent inventory. Not a fan of the navigation.

National Multi List Service – Good online site. I enjoy the ads with video tours.

Cranky Ape – This online site is a bit different on that you need to bid and compete with others on the vehicles in their inventory.

Some other good sources for finding RV's include:

Local papers

Craigslist

Tempest

Facebook Groups - ex. RV Classifieds.

As you can see there's a ton of options out there. Now all you need to do is answer the questions I laid out earlier in this chapter, and determine what features you want and how much you want to spend.

Some Key Features to Consider

Having the right set of features in your RV can make or break your experience. You want to ensure you have the things you need in order to survive and thrive while out on the road. RV living doesn't mean you have to rough it. If you want to lead a minimalist lifestyle you can, but if you still want all the comforts of home on the road, you can have that also.

Here are a few key features to consider when buying your RV

1. Space – If the amount of room available is a key element to your happiness on the road then having a RV with highers ceilings, more leg room, and deeper cabinets might be up your alley. Just remember the more space you have the more expensive it can get. Also, a larger size RV will be harder to drive and navigate then smaller RV's. Some RV parks and roads have size restrictions, so you'll want to take that into consideration.

2. Connectivity – Do you want access to the internet for business and pleasure. Do you want a satellite dish for your TV. Are you looking for a home theater system, a LCD television, satellite radio, or maybe iPod & Mp3 hookups. One thing to consider getting, if you want a lot of these high tech toys, is a Powerline energy management system. It will help to ease the electrical load you'll be putting on your RV.

3. Earth Friendly – Do you want the ability to run off of solar power, have energy efficient appliances, or maybe use wind turbines to power your electronics. If you put a premium on earth friendly options then paying for some of these features might be something you want to consider.

4. Safety – For many of us with families, safety is a priority in our RV. If you feel the same way, then you may want to look into RV's with a strong chassis construction, and higher resistance to the elements and rust. You may want to also make sure your RV comes equipped with air bags, circuit protectors, and electronic monitoring systems that can keep an eye on things like tire pressure and vehicle stability.

5. Driver Convenience – You want as smooth and enjoyable a ride as possible when driving all over the country. One of the areas I focused on in my RV hunt was making sure I had things like GPS, rear vision cameras, reclining bucket seats, and emergency start assistance switches.

6. Floor Plans and Furniture – This will serve as your home, so having a footprint that works for you and your family is crucial. Are high end finishes and high quality furniture something that's important. Do you want more or less appliances for cooking in the kitchen. How many beds do you need? These are all questions you'll want to answer before purchasing.

7. Slide Outs – Just like the name implies, these are extensions that slide out of the side of your RV to give you more room. Some examples of slide outs include, extra bedroom space, extra kitchen space, and extra living room space. Some things to consider with slide outs is they can fail mechanically over time, and cause other issues like leaks and electrical issues. Slide outs offer a lot of convenience, and extra space, but they do present the likelihood of future issues, it's just an issue of what is important to you as a buyer.

8. Fuel Efficiency – RV's are notorious for how much gas they consume. Over the past few years, manufacturers have begun adding more fuel efficiency features that you'll need to consider. For example, you can go with a regular RV, or a hybrid model RV that can get as high as 40% better fuel mileage. You can also go with a RV that weighs less and has a good aerodynamic front profile in order to achieve more fuel efficiency.

Chapter Two: The First Timer's Checklist

In this section, you will find:

- The First Timer's Checklist

The First Timer's Checklist

You've picked our RV, and made a purchase! You've also answered many of the questions I posed above, and have worked on your general overall budget and expenses. You've taken a safety course and upgraded your license. You've also decided on whether you'll be working, and if so what your plan for that entails. You'll also know what you're doing about things like mail, storage and your current property. If you still haven't answered those questions, stop and do so now before continuing on.

Great! Now that you've figured those things out, what's next? Well, in this section I'll go over what I like to call the "First Timer's Checklist". This is basically a list of things you need to do and prepare for before actually hitting the road full time.

Stocking Your RV

Before you head out, you'll need to initially stock your RV with everything you think you'll need while starting out on the road. Here is a list of some essentials to inspire you. There's no way to make a complete list, everyone is different. Think of what is important to you, and you'll probably come up with a bunch of other items you'll want to bring with you.

1. Pillows, pillowcases, blankets, towels & sheets.

2. Plates, pots, pans, silverware, cooking utensils, cups, glasses.

3. Paper towels, tissues, RV toilet paper, garbage bags, storage bags.

4. Shampoo, conditioner, body wash, soap, toothpaste, Q tips.

5. First aid kit – Any medications you're taking, bandages, thermometer, aspirin, tweezers, antibacterial ointment, compress, first aid instruction book, list of emergency contact numbers.

6. Deodorant, cologne / perfume, hair brush, hair dryer, razors, scissors, tape, rubber bands, post it notes, carpet or fake grass for outside steps.

7. Flash lights, batteries (different sizes), bug repellent, pocket knife, nylon cords (different sizes), candles, lanterns, ant spray, ant traps.

8. Coffee pot, toaster, serving tray, kitchen gadgets, pot holders, spatula, small trash can, paper plates and cups, table cloth, measuring cups & spoons, aluminium foil, zip lock bags.

9. Radio (battery and AC operated), broom, dust pan, small vacuum, travel clock, folding chairs, playing cards, games, umbrella, sponge, rags.

10. Propane grill, smaller propane bottles, dish drainer, bungee cords (different sizes), disposable rubber gloves, bubble wrap (for delicate items you don't want broken).

11. Level, light bulbs, garden hose, fire extinguisher, matches, lighters, shovel.

12. Electrical adapters, wheel chocks, black water chemicals, levelling blocks, file folders (hold loose paperwork), awning tie downs, lubricating oil.

13. Fuse puller, extra fuses, electrical extension cord, sewer hose / fittings

14. Water filter, fresh water hose (at least 25 foot), cleaning supplies.

15. Tools (for example, socket sets, wrenches, hammer, screwdrivers, screws, nails, pliers, jack, Ohm meter, jumper cables, tire pressure gauge, axe).

16. Food (coffee, sugar, salt, pepper, condiments, etc.), shoes (multiple pairs).

17. Clothes, personal items, books, magazines, pen, paper, stapler, paper.

18. Proof of insurance / roadside assistance plans, drivers license, other ID, RV & towing registration, maps, owners manuals for RV and appliances.

RV Maintenance Checklist

Before heading out you'll want to make sure you've read and studied your RV owner's manual. Don't be afraid to make some notes of things that will need to be addressed on a routine basis.

Whenever I'm about to leave for a trip, I always run through this list first. I had to learn this one the hard way. I had a few instances where I ended up in a jam because I wasn't checking some basic things in advance. Not only do I check these all before leaving on my trip, I continue to do a thorough inspection at least once a month.

1. Visually inspect all your tires. Check tire pressure on all your tires. You don't want to drive a RV on a flat tire. That's just a recipe for disaster.

2. Start engine. Check idling noise. Check brakes

3. Check all of your clamps and hoses. Look for signs of leaking, and make sure they're all tight and firm. This check also includes any connections that are between your fuel tank and engine.

4. Check your refrigerator flue before beginning it with propane. If you've left your RV stored for awhile, birds or insects could have gotten in and clogged it with a nest. These clogs can lead to fire, or carbon monoxide poisoning.

5. Test out smoke detector.

6. Check water level in batteries.

7. Check fire extinguisher.

8. Test front / rear lights, door windows, door locks, headlights.

9. Test signal lights, emergency flashers, brake lights.

10. Test air conditioner, window defroster, heater, windshield wipers.

11. Check and clean engine compartment.

12. Check all your towing connections.

13. Check to make sure everything is disconnected and stored away properly For example, the water & sewer hoses.

14. Make sure slide outs are slide in.

15. Make sure antenna is down.

16. Make sure your awnings are in.

17. Make sure manual / hydraulic jacks are up.

18. Make sure everything loose in your RV is secured properly.

19. Make sure wheel chocks are removed (if used).

20. Make sure solar panel is flat (if used).

Preparation And Planning

You've stocked up on your supplies and food, you've learned your owner's manual and you have a solid maintenance checklist in place. Next, you need finalize your budgeting, and first trips itinerary. This step can be crucial to your success. Improper planning and budgeting can ruin your dreams of RV living quickly. I'll go more in to depth about budgeting and planning in Chapter 4.

Campground Arrival, Setup & Leaving Breakdown Checklist

You've done all the above and are finally started on your first trip. Now it's time to stop overnight at your first campground. Here is a list of things you'll want to go over and accomplish for the best experience possible.

Arrival

1. Park near the office or entrance.

2. Check yourself in. I always check to see if there's a discount for RV club members like **Escapees** or **Good Sam Club**.

3. Ask for park map and best ways to drive in. Also ask for directions to the park facilities.

4. Check to see if Internet is offered and any details needed to use it.

5. If after hours look for after hours instructions on how to check in. Normally posted by office or entrance.

6. Once checked in, find your RV slot on the park map. Figure out the ideal paths for both entry and exiting.

7. I suggest either walking or taking other transportation to your slot first in order to check for potential issues like tight turns, narrow roads, low trees.

8. Confirm your slot has the facilities you were expecting.

9. Test the water faucet out (especially during winter).

10. If your slot doesn't have sewer facilities then drive over to the dump station to empty out your tanks if needed.

11. If your slot doesn't have water, then drive over to the water source in order to fill up your water tanks.

12. Drive your RV into designated slot. Position RV as you want it, but try being courteous to your new neighbors and don't crowd too closely to their slot.

13. Confirm you can reach all your hookups from where your parked.

14. Deploy all the slides.

15. If towing, unhitch it off your RV.

16. Set your parking brake.

Setting Up

1. Make sure your level. Get level by using either stabilizing jacks or blocks.

2. Put on wheel chocks.

3. Connect yourself to electrical hookup and be sure to switch over the appliances, so you're not draining your own propane or battery.

4. Wearing gloves, hook up sewer hose to the available drain hook up.

5. Lower the stabilizers.

6. Let down your steps and your fold out rail.

7. Tun your AC on (Wait 5 minutes before using).

8. Set up bedroom, kitchen and living room.

9. Uncover the kitchen sink and put away the cover.

10. Turn on your water heater and your water pump.

11. Set up and secure awning.

12. Set up outside items (patio mat, rugs, chairs, tables, etc.).

13. Raise TV antenna (if using).

14. Set up satellite (if using).

15. Set up solar power (if using).

Breaking Down

1. Bring inside your outside items.

2. Lower your TV antenna (if using).

3. Secure satellite (if using).

4. Secure solar power panel (if using).

5. Turn off your water pump and your water heater.

6. Make sure the stove, oven and your pilot light are all out.

7. Turn off radio.

8. Turn off exhaust fan.

9. Make sure that all the water is turned off and nothing is still dripping.

10. Close all your windows.

11. Cover the kitchen sink.

12. Secure and put away all loose items in the interior.

13. Make sure that all doors and cabinets are closed and secured.

14. Check that refrigerator is switched to auto and closed.

15. Turn off the lights.

16. Tun off the AC unit.

17. Put your steps up and be sure to fold in your hand rail.

18. Close and secure the awning.

19. Close the exhaust cover.

20. Disconnect water, sewer and power.

21. Raise all stabilizers.

22. Store the wheel chocks.

23. Attach cables and sway bars.

24. Store blocks and jacks (if used).

25. Lock doors and all storage areas.

26. Make sure campsite is cleaned up, garbage is taken care of, and any fires are doused.

27. Double check all your work.

28. Do a quick safety inspection.

29. Make sure you have everything you'll need for the drive.

Chapter Three: A Brief Guide to RV Legal Considerations & RV Safety

In this section, you will find:

- Legal Considerations to Know Before Heading Out

- Tips for RV Safety

Legal Considerations to Know Before Heading Out

This section will be brief, but it's important nonetheless. Before heading out on the road, you'll want to do your homework on some of the different state laws and statutes concerning RV's. The last thing you want, is getting pulled over, and ticketed, for a reason that could have been easily prevented. Every state has different rules, so you'll want to read up on the state laws for the states you plan on traveling in.

You'll also need to know whether you need an upgraded license for your RV, and the ins and outs of RV registration, RV insurance, RV warranty and RV roadside assistance programs. Things can vary by state, with some states considered to be more RV friendly then others. You'll want to do some research on your own in order to get the right answers for your specific situation. Don't forget to also find out how many hours you're allowed to drive daily. There are restrictions about that.

If you're going out on the road full time you'll also need to know what state you'll be using as your home residence. This is important for things like taxes, registering to vote, renewing your insurance, registration and license.

If you've kept property then you won't have to worry about it. However, if you don't own any residential property, you'll want to look into what state should be considered your home residence. This is an important, and often overlooked thing by newbies.

Tips For RV Safety

Safety is the name of the game when out on the road. Ensuring you and your families well being is paramount. This section will discuss a few of my top tips for safe RV living. If you're new to operating a RV, it can be difficult at first. It's important to practice as much as possible. I recommend taking a RV driving course, if possible.

Top RV Safety Tips

1. Using the maintenance checklist above, I would always inspect your RV top to bottom before leaving any destination. Checking the brakes, tires, fluids and oil levels can save you from an unpleasant breakdown mid trip. I would also inspect for any broken latches, damage to the body of the RV, and broken mirrors.

2. Secure Your Interior – Make sure everything that needs to be secured and locked up is done so. That includes slide outs. I've made this mistake once before and it ended with broken dishes and glasses everywhere.

3. Keep Essential Supplies Stocked – Always have extra batteries, water and food on hand, in case of any breakdowns or issues. It never hurts to be prepared.

4. Keep Propane Tank Maintained – This is very important! You need to understand everything about your propane tank and how to keep it functioning in tip top shape.

5. Have A Route Mapped Out and Take Sufficient Breaks – There are few things worse then getting lost while on the road. Not only that, but it can leave you stranded in unfamiliar areas with nowhere to park come night time. You should also takes breaks at least once every few hours. Driver fatigue is a common cause for accidents. Don't let that be you!

6. Follow 20% Rule – RV vehicles take more time top accelerate and slow down then normal vehicles. Therefore, you need to judge your distance, and give yourself at least 20% longer to do these things in order to stay safe.

7. Be Careful Cornering – Slowly approach any corners. Hitting corners hard in a RV is a recipe for disaster. With practice, you'll become a master at hitting turns safely in no time.

8. Go Easy On The Brakes - Your tires and brakes need to be treated properly. The better you treat them the longer they'll last you.

9. Know The Height Of Your RV – You'd be surprised at how many people crash into low bridges and overhangs because they didn't know the height of their new RV. Don't let that be you!

10. Parking & Backing Up – When I first started this is the area I struggled with the most. You should practice this in open areas as much as you can until you've gotten the hang of it. Don't rush, that's how accidents happen. Always be sure that you can tell where you're going and that others can see you.

Chapter Four: A Guide to RV Expenses – Budgeting & Planning

In this section, you will find:

- A Guide to RV Expenses & Budgeting

- A Guide to RV Planning

RV Expenses & Budgeting

Typical RV Expenses

This section will go over some of the common expenses you will encounter while out traveling full time in your RV. It's vital to know these numbers, as best possible, in advance so you can budget for them properly. If you're determined to live full time on the road, this is one area you cannot afford to not take seriously.

Everyone's budget is different. Each of us has different wants and needs. What is important to some, will not even register for others. Therefore, I'll use the types of expenses I had as an example. Once you've read mine, I suggest you write down your projected types of expenses for the month, as well as any types of variable expenses you may incur during your travels. The more informed you are, the better off you'll be once your actually out on the road.

Typical Monthly Costs

RV Cost – Are you paying a monthly payment or do you own it free and clear.

RV Insurance – Shop around for the best price, and roadside assistance plans. The larger your RV, the bigger the bill each month.

Health Insurance – An important thing many newbies forget to calculate into their monthly expenses before heading out. You need health insurance!

Household Items & Food – Try and figure out these expenditures in advance. I'm sure the numbers will change every month, but try and get as close as possible.

Propane – Shop around for prices. This is a difficult one to gauge until you've been on the road full time for at least a few months, and have learned your monthly usage patterns.

Internet / TV / Phone – If there being used, then you need to account for them.

Mail – How do you get your mail? Do you use a PO Box?

Laundry – You need to wash your clothes. RV parks usually have cheaper facilities then normal laundromats.

Storage – Do you have a storage unit you need to pay for each month with all your old stuff in it.

Subscriptions – I'm a member of certain paid subscription services like Good Sam Club, Netflix, Google Music, Amazon Prime. Basically any service you a pay a monthly or yearly fee to use.

RV Dump – When those reserve tanks get filled they need emptying. Some dump stations are free, but others can cost you a few bucks.

Campground Costs & Parking – Are you staying at free campsites or paid campsites. Try to figure out your destinations far in advance, so you can find out prices, and budget accordingly. Not knowing these costs in advance can seriously wreck your budget.

Tools – I wasn't much of a do it yourself type of guy before hitting the road. This meant my tool box was pretty barren. I try and save a little each month to purchase new tools I may need if I ever break down.

Entertainment – Life is for living. This is your monthly allowance towards going out and enjoying yourself. I try to give myself a fixed amount every month, and then I plan out most of my activities in advance.

Overages – I always set aside an overage fund each month for things like grabbing a drink at a store, or some beef jerky.

Variable Expenses

RV Maintenance – Everything breaks eventually. Be prepared or face the consequences when it happens. I set aside a little each month for monthly maintenance, and actual breakdowns.

Clothes – These don't last forever. At some point you'll need to buy new apparel. I set a small amount aside for my wardrobe.

Diesel – Depending on the amount you drive and fuel prices, this number can jump all over the place. I always map my route out a month or two in advance, to try and estimate the costs as much as I can.

Eating Out – If you enjoy going out to eat, then this is an expense you'll need to try and plan for.

Upgrades – Every year, cool new gadgets are released to make RV living a little more comfortable and fun. If you're like me, and want to buy some new toys every year, then you need to budget for it. I also save up for eventually doing larger upgrades and refurbishments.

RV Budgeting

From all the expenses mentioned above, you can tell there's a lot of different costs that go in to RV living full time on the road. Having a budget in place, will allow you to continuing pursuing your dreams for as long as you desire. Having a solid budget will also help to ease some of the money related stress you may start to feel once out on the road.

There's a bunch of great resources online for how to manage a RV budget. Check out the links below, to help you create your own working monthly budget. Remember to keep detailed records, and track all of your spending. This will allow you to find ways to reduce and eliminate expenses going forward.

1. Gone With The Wynns

2. RV Dreams

3. Wheeling It

4. Technomadia

RV Planning

Planning out your trip in advance is a key element to a successful trip. I always try and plan a few months in advance to make budgeting easier.

Here are some online sites that can help you plan your next trip easier. Some of these are free and some are paid services. Use whichever ones you feel comfortable with, or plan your trip the old fashioned way by yourself.

RV Trip Wizard - Great site for trip planning but costs $39 a year to join.

Good Sam Club - Another good option. Free for Good Sam Club members.

Road Trip America – Good free planning resource.

USCAmpgrounds – Good free planning resource

Ultimate Campgrounds - Good free planning resource

Chapter Five: A Guide to RV Food Prep & Storage

In this section, you will find:

- Guide to RV Food Prep

- Guide to RV Food Storage

Once you hit the road, eating out every meal will get old quick. That's why RV food prep and storage is such an integral part to your every day life out on the road. Having easy systems put in place to handle food prep and storage enables you to use your limited kitchen space as efficiently as possible.

Guide to RV Food Prep

1. Get your groceries in one trip and prepare your meals for the week.

2. Get some RV specific prep tools. They can make life easier on the road. You can find them online or at any camping store.

3. Containers need to be both microwaveable and freezer safe.

4. If something smells off, throw it out. Don't risk illness on food gone bad.

5. Never put hot food in the freezer. That can lead to the growth of harmful bacteria. Always let your food cool down to room temp. This will also allow for the food to have room to properly expand once frozen.

6. Know your freezer fill level. You want your freezer always running at its best.

7. Label and track all meals. It will let you find what you want easier, while also allowing you know which items need to be restocked and when.

8. Always under cook vegetables slightly. This way once you reheat them, they don't get musty and disgusting.

9. Once a food is defrosted do not refreeze. Not only can this cause bacteria to grow, but your food won't retain it's original good flavors.

10. Stock up on spices. Nothing makes food more flavorful then a wide array of different spices.

11. Make foods that are easy to clean up once finished. Space is limited. You don't want to be turning your small kitchen space into a nightmare.

12. Try cooking one dish meals with an easy to make side. Most RV kitchen spaces aren't meant for gourmet cooking. Trying pairing one dish with a simple salad or other side you can easily put together.

13. Use paper plates, plastic cups and disposable utensils whenever possible. Why make clean up harder then it needs to be. Disposable plates and cups cut your clean up time in half.

Guide to RV Food Storage

1. Be creative! Space is limited so think outside the box. Kitchen stuff doesn't need to live only in the kitchen. If you've got room for it elsewhere, store it there and bring it out when needed.

2. Never use round containers. There terrible for stacking and end up costing you space.

3. Resealable zip lock bags are awesome. You can empty bigger boxes and containers into these bags and save a ton of space.

4. Try installing clamps, hooks, and organizers on the back of your cabinet doors. This will allow you to be better organized, and add more usable space to the kitchen.

5. Buy only what you need. Hit the store every week and only get what you need for that weeks meals and snacks. Advanced preparation is key! It will make life much easier in the long run. I always bring a grocery list to the store

6. Learn to organize like a professional. Packing your refrigerator and freezer is an art form. Think of it like a puzzle or a game of Tetris. The only way you win is if everything fits nicely together. This might take some time to master, but trust me you will. I used to have horrible organizational skills. After about 4 months on the road I was a whiz.

7. Go online to sites like Pinterest for inspiration on how to save space. You'll be amazed with some of the things people have come up with. Take your favorite ideas and incorporate them into your RV kitchen.

What Items I Keep In My RV Kitchen

Here are some of the things I carry with me on the road, and keep stored in my RV kitchen. I like to cook so I carry more than most might. I've found that with the items below I can cook most anything I want. I'm also not averse to traveling with glass. I wrap all my glass carefully before driving so I haven't had any real issues with things breaking. I know for some this might be too much of a hassle. I suggest doing whatever is comfortable for you.

On the subject of pots and pans, be sure to get a good set. You'll be kicking yourself otherwise. I suggest not going with a lightweight set. If you need to conserve weight on the RV, do it elsewhere. This list came together over time. It started off much smaller, and as I got more comfortable in the smaller kitchen space I started adding and experimenting.

- 10 inch frying pan and lid
- Dutch oven and lid
- 2 quart pot and lid
- 2 quart casserole dish
- 4 quart stainless steel pot and lid
- 4 quart pot and lid
- 5 quart roaster
- 6 quart crock pot
- 6 inch cast iron skillet
- 16 quart stockpot (For soups and steaming seafood)
- 2-3 cup food processor

- Hand held electric mixer
- Mini Blender
- 2 smaller platters
- 2 big serving bowls
- Toaster oven
- Spice rack

- Various sized disposable aluminum baking pans

Chapter Six: 100+ Tips to Make Life On The Road Easier

In this section, you will find:

- 100+ Tips to Make Life On The Road Easier

100 + Tips to Make Life On The Road Easier

1. Mount any electrical adapters in order to keep them organized and neat.

2. Use one of your dry food containers as a mini garbage can.

3. Bubble wrap is great for insulating windows during the winter months.

4. To keep flies at bay wipe down everything using Pine-Sol.

5. Get yourself a dry erase board. Can be used to keep emergency and campground information on hand for each new location you're at.

6. Velcro is a great for holding in place your black out curtains.

7. Command hooks are excellent for hanging up your curtains.

8. Line all your drawers and shelves with a non slip liner.

9. Use tape that glows in the dark on your entry / exit stairs. Helps with visibility at night.

10. Keep out wasps with old flea collars that have been cut up. Cut the collar in two and place in any compartments where propane is stored. Wasps go crazy for the taste and smell of propane.

11. Not sure why, but a bar of soap called Irish Spring helps to keep any mice out of the RV.

12. Using a rod in your shower will allow you to hang up clothes that are still not dry.

13. Mesh sleeves are great for keeping items from clanging together like wine bottles.

14. Spray paint is a great tool for touching up any plastic areas on the RV that got sun faded over time.

15. Glad Press n' Seal will easily turn any cup into a nice travel cup. Just pop a hole in the top with your straw, and you're good to go.

16. Anti fatigue mats are great for insulation and added comfort when used on the bottom of sleeping bunks.

17. Install a towel rod in order to keep all your bathroom products stored safely in one place. Just place the items between the rod and the wall for secure storage.

18. Collapsible laundry baskets are great as temporary garbage cans when at your camping site.

19. If you don't want to constantly wrap up your glasses in bubble wrap while traveling, try sliding a koozie over them. Will dramatically decrease the chance of the glasses hitting each other hard enough to break.

20. Always keep duct tape and clothespins handy. These can be used in a variety of different ways.

21. Buy a flashlight hat. It can come in handy out on the road. Whether getting to the facilities during the middle of the night in your campground, or fixing something outdoors at night you'll be glad you got one.

22. Buy a stick lighter. This is an essential tool. Great for lighting campfires, pilot lights and grills. Makes those jobs simple.

23. Buy a clear elbow to put on your sewer. It allows you to see everything going on in your sewer and also allows you to backwash your system and make sure things are getting drained properly. Not a pretty thing, but a necessary one.

24.   Buy a good set of headphones. This holds true especially if on the road with other people. RV's are tight spaces and having a good set of headphones will allow you to escape one another when you need some alone time.

25.   Buy a good folding chair. You'll be using them a ton around the campfire so get ones that are comfortable. Always get an extra chair or two. This serves two purposes. Makes a great backup if one gets broken and also you can set out an extra chair to encourage new campground neighbors to stop and sit for a bit.

26.   Buy an Extend-A-Shower. In the majority of RV's shower space is almost laughable. If you've got a curtain in your shower, then an extender will give you a good amount more room. I'm not a tiny man so this one was a must have for my RV.

27.   Buy a nice tablet. These are great for a multitude of reasons. They've become relatively inexpensive, they take up very little room, and they offer a ton of entertainment value. You can play games, listen to music, watch video, read books, write, work and surf the internet all from the same device. I also have a laptop and cloud printer with me but I work part time from the road.

28.   Buy a small fan that comes with a nice sized extension cord. You can get one that runs off batteries, but I've had less success with those types over the years. Either way they're great for hot nights, and quite frankly I can't even sleep at night unless I have the sound of wind blowing in my ear.

29.   Buy an electric blanket and a sleeping bag, for those extra cold winter nights. Will help to save from running the heater all night long.

30.   Buy either a bike or small electric scooter. Great for getting around larger campgrounds and small towns without having to navigate the RV. Bikes are also great for daily exercise and seeing some nature.

31. Purchasing an aerodynamic RV can save you a ton of money in the amount of fuel you'll buy over the lifetime of the RV.

32.   Traveling with pets requires work and patience but is completely worth it.

33.   Solar power is awesome. It works and you should strongly consider getting it.

34.   Always keep your tanks full. Getting stuck in traffic with low gas reserves has stressed me out more times than I'd like to remember.

35.   If you don't want to pay for Internet in your RV, places like libraries, FedEx Kinko's, and KOA Kampgrounds are excellent places to go online.

36.   Be careful with your medications. If they cause drowsiness don't drive while on them.

37.   Don't go without a cell phone or satellite phone. RV living off the grid can be great, but having a cell phone has saved me in quite a few jams over the years, especially if your RV living full time.

38.   Portable space heaters are good for cold nights when temperatures dip. They can help your propane furnace from getting overworked.

39.   Having a water filter on your RV is a must in my eyes.

40.   High beams don't do a damn thing when traveling in fog. I usually try to find a safe place to park and call it a night. RV's are too big to be driving around blindly.

41. Always check rubber seals around windows and doors. You want to replace them if they're looking worn. It can lead to unpleasant water leaks if you don't stay on top of it.

42.   I always use two pairs of shoes. One for inside the RV and one for outside the RV. Helps cut down on tracking in dirt and mud.

43.   If you have a roof leak check your air conditioner right away. I always check all the bolts and seals. Most of the time this is the area causing the issue.

44.   In winter, I always weather strip, use more rugs and heavier curtains for better insulation.

45.   WD40 is your friend. Always have some in the RV.

46.   Driving in hotter weather is hard on the RV. Try traveling in the early morning and late afternoon to minimize the impact.

47.   Realize it can take your RV almost the length of a football field sometimes to stop completely. Always give yourself plenty of room. Especially during rain or snow.

48.   When backing up always go nice and slow. Don't try rushing when driving in reverse your only asking for trouble.

49.   Be nice to your RV plumbing. Get RV toilet paper and keep up on the maintenance.

50.   Get your engine serviced at least once every year. I would also clean the engine at least once a year.

51. On the road some of the best food I've ever had has been at greasy spoons and roadside diners. Be sure to experience it for yourself.

52.   Keep your roof clean. It will lengthen the life of the roof tremendously. I routinely clean my roof 3 times a year.

53.   Get a slide topper to keep debris and moisture out of slide out rooms.

54.   I spent more to get cruise control, a nice stereo, and electronic mirrors. Let's just say it turned out to be a great decision. One I recommend you considering.

55.   Get your chassis rustproofed. It's a smart way to protect the foundation of your RV.

56.   Know how to read a map properly. This will save you a lot of time.

57. Clean the entire interior of your RV thoroughly at least 3-4 times a year. Clean the AC, furnace, drawers, floors, walls and compartments. Helps to keep out bugs and just makes your RV a nice place to live in.

58.   Protect any sensitive information. I use an encrypted thumb drive to store all my important information. I also have two backup copies, one of which stays with my family who are not on the road. I also back up anything important to my Amazon Cloud Drive and my Google Drive. I like to have multiple backs up because I got burned once before.

59.   Buy a portable tank-less air compressor. This is a great item for fixing flat tires on bikes, topping off your spare tire and inflating items. For example, I have an inner tube for those lazy summer days on the river.

60.   Join some RV clubs and associations. They offer a lot of wonderful benefits and networking opportunities. Well worth the money I spent on them.

61. Add extra battery capacity to your RV. This will allow you to go further off the grid to those hard to get to spots, for longer periods of time.

62.   I installed a Fantastic Vent Fan in my RV and I love it. It does a good job of cooling the RV and removing unwanted food odor, among other things.

63. Install a good surge protector.

64. Install a good digital thermometer. Mine was garbage, so I immediately changed it out with a better one.

65. Get unique set of locks for your RV. There are many dishonest people in the world. I prefer to be careful instead of being sorry.

66. Upgrade your shower head and faucets. I got the Oxygenics brand fixtures and I've been very pleased with them.

67. Invest in a portable ice cube maker. No more trips into town for ice!

68. Have a reflective vest in your RV in case of a roadside emergency at night.

69. Buy a temperature gun. So many handy uses. Great for checking tire temp, brakes temps, how well your AC is working, checking your grill temp, refrigerator temp, freezer temp and oven temp.

70. During winter use heat strips on your fresh water hose and then cover it with a foam insulation. Stops water from freezing and damaging your pipes and plumbing.

71. During winter keep the waste valves closed when not in use and keep them covered with insulation.

72. Only dump tanks when they are full. Helps reduce the chances of freezing. I also add a splash of antifreeze.

73. During winter keep a heating pad handy. Good for warming up pipes.

74. Have a shovel on your RV. If you ever get caught in the snow you'll need to dig yourself out.

75. Get a portable power washer for cleaning your RV. Makes the job go a lot quicker.

76. When traveling spend some time in each location and get to know what the area has to offer. You're on the road to experience new things. Don't lose sight of that.

77. When planning your route try and avoid toll routes to save some money.

78. Many parks offer deals where you can camp at the park for free if you put in some volunteer work hours.

79. Call the chamber of commerce for towns you'll be going to. Often they can let you know of any interesting activities going on while you're in town. They will also sometimes offer you free coupons for businesses in town or events in town.

80. Camping world and most Walmart's are alright with you parking in their lots overnight. Some motels and rest stops are also fine with you parking in their lots. I usually ask permission just in case. If you don't want to do that I suggest using some discretion. Don't pull out all your slide outs, leave early in the morning and don't cause a scene.

81. Learn how to perform general maintenance on your RV, if you ever get stuck somewhere you'll be better prepared to handle the situation.

82. Keep spare parts like ignition coils, air filters, spark plugs, fan belts, water hose belts, wires and a soldering iron on your RV. At some point you'll be glad you did.

83. If somewhere looks too small to drive through or park in it probably is. I've rolled the dice before and it always comes up snake eyes.

84. When traveling to go somewhere make sure that the place is open when you get there. I've had this happen to me once before where I traveled out of my way to see something and it was closed. Now I know to always double check before heading off.

85. Know the weight of your RV. You don't want to let it get overloaded.

86. Try to drive under 400 miles a day. Any more and you're starting to push it.

87. Your cockpit can't get too comfortable. Driving for long periods can be difficult so the space around you should be as comfortable as possible.

88. Always check your carbon monoxide, smoke and LP gas detectors on a regular basis.

89. A nice set of mud flaps will help to keep any debris off the RV.

90. When you're not at the RV use an on-board timer system to trick would be thieves.

91. In order for you refrigerator to work optimally your RV must be level.

92. CB chatter can help you determine upcoming traffic and weather issues when traveling. They also make a good companion when bored.

93. If you don't like a campground or spot you're in go somewhere else. There's no need to tough it (unless there's inclement weather).

94. Keep a roll of quarters handy in your shower kit. You never know when you'll hit a campground with pay showers.

95. If you're traveling with other adults, teach them to drive the RV so you can lessen the burden of driving on yourself.

96. When tackling hard uphill areas be sure to go down the hill in the same gear you went up it.

97. When deciding on a back up camera for your RV, be sure to make sure it works in the dark. If it doesn't, it won't do you any good half the time you need it.

98. Change out your windshield wipers bi-annually.

99. I got an electronically operated awning and I love it. You should check them out.

100. It's not a real camping trip without some a few delicious s'mores.

Chapter Seven: My Favorite Spots Travel Guide

In this section, you will find:

- My Favorite Spots Travel Guide

My Favorite Spots Travel Guide

Not all destinations are equal. A lot of it has to do with personal preference. Some people will enjoy lavish campgrounds with flashy amenities, while others will enjoy off the grid locations with access to greater wildlife and scenic views.

In this section I'll go over a few of my favorite spots. Some of these made the list because of the RV parks themselves, while others made it for their location and activities the area had to offer.

1. Yellowstone National Park – Located primarily in Wyoming. It's the flagship park for a reason. Beautiful scenery and a ton of great campgrounds to choose from no matter what your budget. I got to see the Old Faithful geyser, and a ton of interesting wildlife during my time visiting.

2. Crater Lake National Park – Located in Klamath, Oregon. One of the most beautiful spots I ever had the privilege of visiting. The bluest water and incredible sheer cliffs. It was a sight to behold.

3. Horse Thief Lake – A campground Located In Hill City, South Dakota, and one of my favorite spots to visit due to its proximity to both Custer Stater Park and Mt. Rushmore. This RV park has lots of old time charm. It offered shops for your basic supplies, as well as fire rings for each site and a heated pool.

4. Blue Ridge Parkway – This is a huge park located in both Virginia & North Carolina. Tons of scenic vistas, mountain ranges and old farmsteads make this an amazing place to visit and see for yourself.

5. Durango RV Resort – This is a RV park in Red Bluff, California. In this campground you'll find a lot of higher end amenities. Every site has Powerhouse Pedestals. These are great for allowing you to have cable TV, electricity, and high speed WiFi. This RV resort also comes with pools, outdoor fireplaces, a nice clubhouse, and a dog park for your animals. If you're looking to camp in style this is a place you'll enjoy.

6. Arches National Park – Located in Grand County, Utah. Arches is a beautiful park that holds over 2000 naturally preserved sandstone arches. There are tons of different landscapes and colors to take in when visiting this park.

7. Rivers Edge RV Park – This park is located in Fairbanks, Alaska. It offers gorgeous scenery and a ton of outdoor activities. These include hiking and biking trails, as well as fishing and hunting. They even offer shuttle buses into town so you can keep your RV hooked up at the campground.

8. Grand Canyon National Park – Located in Mohave, Arizona. You need to travel to the Grand Canyon at least once in your lifetime. It's magnificent. I actually took a helicopter ride through the Grand Canyon (we even landed in the Canyon and had lunch). We also went over the Hoover Dam. Overall it was an incredible experience.

9. Boyd's Key West RV Park – Located in Key West, Florida. A great waterfront RV park that is right near town and all the fun Key West has to hold. The park has both a pool and beach area. It even has its own marina. This is a popular spot among travelers but well worth the trip.

10. Fort Wilderness, Disney World - Located in Lake Buena Vista, Florida. They offer a nice campground if you ever wanted to visit Disney World without having to stay in a hotel. My family loved it here. They offer a bunch of amenities and activities, plus Disney World itself. Great for family vacations!

Chapter Eight: A Guide to Earning Money From The Road

In this section, you will find:

- A Guide to Earning Money From The Road

For many of us, the idea of RV living full time seems like a dream that will never be within our grasp. Unless you've come into some money or saved for years until retired, how is someone able to live on the road with no steady job income. Well, I'm happy to report it's completely possible. It will take some work and a lot of planning / budgeting but it's completely do-able. This section will discuss many different ways you can earn money while out on the road full time.

A Guide to Earning Money From The Road

If you're like I was and want to live a RV lifestyle but still need an income, this section is for you. Whether you want to work part time or full time, I'll go over some ideas and opportunities you can use to your advantage. There are endless ways to earn a buck if you get creative. Here a few of my personal favorites, some of which I use myself to this day.

1. Try workamping. What's that you ask? Well, it's a popular term referring to people who work at spots like RV parks, resorts, motels, hotels, amusement parks and other similar jobs in order to get free parking, utilities and additional wages. These jobs are usually seasonal and while some are good, many complain about the rate of pay and amount of work required. I don't do this one anymore, but I did when first starting out. I've built up other streams of income over the years to avoid doing work that requires manual labor. I get enough of a workout maintaining my RV.

2. Become a Freelancer – If you have writing skills, technical skills, and design skills you can easily find work on sites like Elance or Upwork. These sites allow people like us to work online and use our skills to make some additional money. When first starting out you need to gain some experience so it may take a while to get the ball rolling. However, once you've earned a good reputation you can make a nice amount of money each month.

3. Virtual Assistant – There are companies out there that need virtual assistants and will pay a premium for qualified applicants. This was never my cup of tea so I don't have personal experience with it, but I've met others who've made a good income from working this way.

4. Start an eBay or Amazon business – For living on the road I prefer Amazon FBA (Fulfilled by Amazon), but you can do whatever you're comfortable with. I make a few thousand a month using these sites. I'm always traveling so I take the opportunity to buy and resell items I find deals on along the way. I love going to yard sales, flea markets and thrift stores so this one doesn't even feel like work most of the time. The great thing about Amazon FBA is you can send your items in to Amazon and they'll handle everything from shipping to the customer to handling communications and returns.

5. Start another type of online business. I know people who create and monetize niche websites. I also know people who create digital products or courses and sell them online. Get creative! There's lot of opportunity in starting your own business.

6. Telecommute – Before you quit your old job, see if they'll allow you to telecommute from the road. More and more companies are offering this option with the advances in technology over the past few years.

7. If you're a skilled laborer sell your skills on the road. You can offer your services on Craigslist for the area you're visiting in.

8. Sell at Flea Markets – Maybe you don't want to sell your items online. You can still sell at flea markets. Almost every area has at least one, and there a great way to pick up some extra fast cash.

9. Sell Your Photography – Traveling the country will give you the opportunity to take amazing pictures. If you

enjoy photography try turning it into something that will earn you some extra money.

10. Sell Your Musical Talent – If you're a singer or musician try and book gigs to places you'll be visiting.

11. Start a YouTube channel or a blog – It will take some time to build a following but many people have great success in these mediums.

Chapter Nine: The Ultimate RV Resource Guide

In this section, you will find:

- The Ultimate RV Resource Guide

The Ultimate RV Resource Guide

Here is a list of sites and resources I have found to be extremely helpful over the course of my travels. I'm sure I've forgotten a few, but these should be able to help you out a great deal. Some of these are free sites while other are paid sites that I've been a member of in the past or am a member of currently.

You don't need to check these all out at once. Take your time and look at them when you have some free time.
I apologize if any links are outdated. I always try and update this list every few months but sometimes in-between a site will go down or one will slip past me.

Boondockers Welcome
Campendium
Coast to Coast
Cool Works
Escapees RV Club
Find Fuel Stops
Free Campgrounds
Fuelbook
Gas Buddy
Geeks On Tour

Good Sam Club
Harvest Hosts
IRV2 Forums
Mile By Mile Road Trip
Overnight RV Parking
Passport America
Roadside America
Roadtrippers
RV.net Forums
RV Basic Training
RV Buddy
RV Dreams – 3 Budgeting Examples
RV Dump
RV Full Timers Facebook Group
RV Mobile Internet Resource Center
RV Network
RV Park Reviews
RV Parking
RV Parky
RV Service Reviews
RVer Insurance Exchange
Safe Travel USA
Technomadia
Thousand Trails
Travellers Point
Truck Miles
Ultimate Campgrounds
USCAmpgrounds
Work at KOA
Workamper News
Workamping Jobs
Workers On Wheels
Working Couples

Conclusion

You've reached the end! Thank you again for purchasing my book "RV Living Full Time: 100+ Amazing Tips, Secrets, Hacks & Resources to Motorhome Living".

I hope you've gotten a lot out of this book and realize what it takes to lead a RV lifestyle. Living on the road is a rewarding experience. At times it can be a struggle, and driving in bad weather can be a bit nerve wracking. However, I wouldn't change my life for the anything.

Remember to get all your research done in advance. Making the right decisions initially will make your life at lot easier down the line. I had to learn that one the hard way. Fortunately I was able to adjust and our RV is now a well oiled machine.

I wish you and your family good luck and the adventure of a lifetime!

Made in the USA
San Bernardino, CA
14 August 2018